Kressmann Taylor

Address Unknown

Mit einem Vorwort von
Charles Douglas Taylor

Herausgegeben von
Susanne Lenz

Philipp Reclam jun. Stuttgart

Diese Ausgabe darf nur in der Bundesrepublik Deutschland, in Österreich und in der Schweiz vertrieben werden.

RECLAMS UNIVERSAL-BIBLIOTHEK Nr. 9107
Alle Rechte vorbehalten
Copyright für diese Ausgabe
© 2003 Philipp Reclam jun. GmbH & Co. KG, Stuttgart
Copyright © für den Text 1938 Kressmann Taylor. Copyright renewed
© 1966 C. Douglas Taylor. Abdruck mit Genehmigung von Simon &
Schuster, Inc., New York
Gesamtherstellung: Reclam, Ditzingen. Printed in Germany 2011
RECLAM, UNIVERSAL-BIBLIOTHEK und RECLAMS
UNIVERSAL-BIBLIOTHEK sind eingetragene Marken
der Philipp Reclam jun. GmbH & Co. KG, Stuttgart
ISBN 978-3-15-009107-4

www.reclam.de

Foreword

When "Address Unknown" was first published in the
United States, in *Story* magazine in September 1938,
it caused an immediate sensation. Written as a series
5 of letters between a Jewish American living in San
Francisco and his former business partner who had
returned to Germany, the story, early on, exposed the
poison of Nazism to the American public.

Within ten days of publication, the entire printing
10 of that issue of *Story* was sold out, and enthusiastic
readers were mimeographing copies of the story to
send to friends. National radio commentator Walter
Winchell heartily recommended the story as "the best
piece of the month, something you shouldn't miss,"
15 and *Reader's Digest* put aside its long-standing no-fic-
tion rule to reprint the piece for its more than three
million readers.

In 1939, Simon & Schuster published *Address Unknown* as a book and sold fifty thousand copies – a
20 huge number in those years. Hamish Hamilton fol-
lowed suit in England with a British edition, and
foreign translations were begun. But 1939 was also
the year of *Blitzkrieg*; within months most of Europe
was under the domination of Adolf Hitler, the Dutch

---

11 **to mimeograph:** (Schrift) vervielfältigen, (Abzüge) herstellen, (Ko-
   pien) anfertigen.
15 **long-standing:** langjährig, seit langem bestehend, alt.
23 **"Blitzkrieg":** Bezeichnung für die zu Beginn des Zweiten
   Weltkriegs 1939 innerhalb kurzer Zeit entschiedenen Feldzüge,
   speziell Hitlers Überfall auf Polen.
24 **domination:** Herrschaft, Gewalt.

3

translation disappeared, and the only other European appearance of *Address Unknown* was on the *Reichskommissar's* list of banned books. So the story remained unknown on the Continent for the next sixty
5 years, despite its great impact and success in the United States and England.

Author Kressmann Taylor, "the woman who jolted America," was born Kathrine Kressmann in Portland, Oregon, in 1903. After graduating from the Univer-
10 sity of Oregon in 1924, she moved to San Francisco and worked as an advertising copywriter, writing for some small literary journals in her spare time. In 1928 the editors of the *San Francisco Review*, a magazine she particularly liked, invited her to a party, where
15 she met Elliott Taylor, the owner of his own advertising agency, and they were married within two weeks. When the Great Depression hit the advertising industry, the couple bought a small farm in southern Oregon. Taking their two small children and adding a
20 third in 1935, they literally "lived off the land," growing their own food and panning for gold.

In 1938 they moved to New York, where Elliott worked as an editor and Kathrine finished writing

---

2f. **Reichskommissar:** Regierungsbeauftragter für die Erfüllung von Verwaltungsaufgaben im Deutschen Reich zwischen 1871 und 1945; von 1933 an in den zur Realisierung des totalitären Herrschaftssystems der Nationalsozialisten entscheidenden Positionen in Staat und Gesellschaft tätig.

7 **to jolt s.o.:** jdn. aufrütteln, -schrecken, erschüttern, jdm. einen Schock versetzen.

11 **advertising copywriter:** Werbetexter(in).

17 **Great Depression:** (Welt-)Wirtschaftskrise nach dem New Yorker Börsenkrach 1929.

21 **to pan for gold:** Gold waschen.

"Address Unknown." Elliott showed it to *Story* magazine editor Whit Burnett, who immediately wished to
publish it. He and Elliott decided that the story was
"too strong to appear under the name of a woman,"
and assigned Kathrine the literary pseudonym *Kressmann Taylor*, a professional name she accepted and
kept for the rest of her life, largely because of the success of *Address Unknown*. This is how she describes
the original motivation for the story:

A short time before the war, some cultivated, in-
tellectual, warmhearted German friends of mine
returned to Germany after living in the United
States. In a very short time they turned into sworn
Nazis. They refused to listen to the slightest criti-
cism about Hitler. During a return visit to Califor-
nia, they met an old, dear friend of theirs on the
street who had been very close to them and who
was a Jew. They did not speak to him. They turned
their backs on him when he held his hands out to
embrace them. How can such a thing happen? *I*
wondered. What changed their hearts so? What
steps brought them to such cruelty?

These questions haunted me very much and I
could not forget them. It was hard to believe that
these people whom I knew and respected had
fallen victim to the Nazi poison. I began research-
ing Hitler and reading his speeches and the writ-
ings of his advisors. What I discovered was terrify-

---

23 **to haunt s.o.:** jdn. verfolgen, umtreiben, jdm. keine Ruhe lassen.
26f. **to research s.o.:** über jdn. recherchieren.
28f. **terrifying:** erschreckend, beängstigend.

ing. What worried me most was that no one in America was aware of what was happening in Germany and they also did not care. In 1938, the isolationist movement in America was strong; the politicians said that affairs in Europe were none of our business and that Germany was fine. Even Charles Lindbergh came back from Germany saying how wonderful the people were. But some students who had returned from studying in Germany told the truth about the Nazi atrocities. When their fraternity brothers thought it would be fun to send them letters making fun of Hitler, they wrote back and said, "Stop it. We're in danger. These people don't fool around. You could murder one of these Nazis by writing letters to him."

When that incident occurred, it rated only a small article in the news, but it caught Elliott's eye; he brought it home to Kathrine, and it gave rise to their joint idea of using a letter as a weapon. She took that idea and went to work on the story she wanted to write.

I wanted to write about what the Nazis were doing and show the American public what happens to real, living people swept up in a warped ideology.

---

4 **isolationist:** isolationistisch, auf (politische) Isolation und Bündnisfreiheit bedacht, bestrebt, sich (außenpolitisch) nicht einzumischen.
7 **Lindbergh:** Charles L. (1902–74), amerikanischer Flieger, der 1927 den ersten Alleinflug über den Atlantik durchführte.
10 **atrocities:** Gräueltaten, Verbrechen.
11 **fraternity brother:** Kommilitone (*fraternity:* studentische Verbindung).
16 **to rate** (infml.): verdienen, wert sein.
23 **to sweep s. o. up:** (fig.) jdn. hinwegfegen, mitreißen.
    warped: pervertiert.

The result was "Address Unknown," a great success about which *The New York Times Book Review* stated in 1939, "This modern story is perfection itself. It is the most effective indictment of Nazism to appear in fiction." That indictment continued in Kathrine's nex book, *Until That Day*, published in 1942.

Following the war, when further indictment of the Nazis no longer seemed necessary, *Address Unknown* slipped from public notice and was largely forgotten, other than its inclusion in an occasional anthology. Elliott Taylor died in 1953, and Kathrine lived as a widow for the next fifteen years, continuing to write and to teach writing, journalism, and humanities at Gettysburg College, in Pennsylvania. Retiring in 1966, she moved to Florence, Italy, where she experienced the great flood of the Arno river in November of that year – which inspired her third book, *Diary of Florence in Flood*, published to critical acclaim in England and America the following spring.

En route to Italy in 1966 on the Italian Line's *Michelangelo*, Kathrine met the American sculptor John Rood. The two felt an immediate attraction, had a shipboard romance, and were married the following year in Minneapolis, where he made his home. Thereafter, they lived part of each year in Minneapolis and part in the Val de Pea, outside Florence. Even after Rood's death in 1974, Kathrine kept both homes for

4 **indictment:** Anklage.
10 **inclusion:** Aufnahme, Einbeziehung.
13 **humanities:** Geisteswissenschaften.
18 **acclaim:** Anerkennung, Beifall.
20 **en route** (adv.): unterwegs, auf dem Weg.
21 **sculptor:** Bildhauer.

nearly twenty years, living quietly in each six months a year, simply as Mrs. John Rood.

Then, in 1995, when Kathrine was ninety-one years old, Story Press reissued *Address Unknown* "to commemorate the 50th anniversary of the liberation of the concentration camps" and because, as *Story* editor Lois Rosenthal wrote, its "significant and timeless message" had earned it "a permanent place in the bookshelves" of America. The book was well received, and Kathrine, happily signing copies and granting television and press interviews, was gratified at its re-emergence, this time with the status of an American literary classic.

Kathrine Kressmann Taylor Rood died in July 1996, late in her ninety-third year, sharp-witted, perceptive, and enthusiastic, even about the end of life. "Dying," she said in her last week, "is normal. It's as normal as being born." And she was ready. She had lived several successful lives: as a wife and mother, as a popular professor, and as the author of three books and a dozen short stories, one of which, *Address Unkown*, was recognized as a classic while she lived.

Shortly after her death, a copy of the 1995 reissue came into the hands of French publisher Henri Dougier of Editions Autrement, Paris. He saw at once its relevance to the entire European community, both those members who had lived under Nazi domination

---

4 **to reissue:** wieder veröffentlichen, wieder abdrucken, neu auflegen.

4f. **to commemorate s.th.:** einer Sache gedenken, an etwas erinnern.

5 **liberation:** Befreiung.

11 **to be gratified at s.th.:** sich über etwas freuen.

11f. **re-emergence:** Wiederkehr; hier auch: Wiederentdeckung.

15f. **perceptive:** einfühlsam.

and those who needed to know what it had been like. He determined that a French translation must be undertaken, and that translation, by Michèle Lévy-Bram, hit the French bestseller list in late 1999. Fifty thousand copies sold that first year, and another fifty thousand in the early months of 2000; the book was selling far more than it ever had in the United States. And other Europeans were reading it, calling for its translation and publication in their own languages: Spanish, Catalan, Italian, Portuguese. I am most gratified that my mother lived long enough to see this little book recognized as the classic it's become. And I know that she and her German ancestors would be delighted that this edition by Reclams Universal-Bibliothek will enable German pupils in the classroom to read *Address Unknown*.

CHARLES DOUGLAS TAYLOR,
SON OF KATHRINE KRESSMANN TAYLOR

---

13 **ancestors:** Vorfahren.

November 12, 1932

Herrn Martin Schulse
Schloss Rantzenburg
Munich, Germany

My Dear Martin:

Back in Germany! How I envy you! Although I have not seen it since my school days, the spell of *Unter den Linden* is still strong upon me – the breadth of intellectual freedom, the discussions, the music, the lighthearted comradeship. And now the old Junker spirit, the Prussian arrogance and militarism are gone. You go to a democratic Germany, a land with a deep culture and the beginnings of a fine political freedom. It will be a good life. Your new address is impressive and I rejoice that the crossing was so pleasant for Elsa and the young sprouts.

As for me, I am not so happy. Sunday morning finds me a lonely bachelor without aim. My Sunday home is now transported over the wide seas. The big

---

9 **spell:** magischer Bann, Zauber, Reiz.
12 **lighthearted:** unbekümmert, unbeschwert.
   comradeship: Kameradschaft.
13 **Prussian:** preußisch.
17 **to rejoice:** sich freuen, große Freude empfinden.
18 **sprout:** Sprössling.

old house on the hill – your welcome that said the day was not complete until we were together again! And our dear jolly Elsa, coming out beaming, grasping my hand and shouting "Max, Max!" and hurrying indoors
5 to open my favorite *Schnapps*. The fine boys, too, especially your handsome young Heinrich; he will be a grown man before I set eyes upon him again.

And dinner – shall I evermore hope to eat as I have eaten? Now I go to a restaurant and over my lonely
10 roast beef come visions of *gebackner Schinken* steaming in its Burgundy sauce, of *Spatzle*, ah! of *Spatzle* and *Spargel!* No, I shall never again become reconciled to my American diet. And the wines, so carefully slipped ashore from the German boats, and the
15 pledges we made as the glasses brimmed for the fourth and fifth and sixth times.

Of course you are right to go. You have never become American despite your success here, and now that the business is so well established you must take your
20 sturdy German boys back to the homeland to be educated. Elsa too has missed her family through the long years and they will be glad to see you as well. The impecunious young artist has now become the family benefactor, and that too will give you a quiet little triumph.
25 The business continues to go well. Mrs. Levine has bought the small Picasso at our price, for which I con-

---

12 f. **to become reconciled to s. th.:** sich mit etwas aus-, versöhnen, abfinden.
15 **pledge:** Treueschwur; Trinkspruch.
  to brim: bis zum Rand gefüllt, randvoll sein, überquellen.
20 **sturdy:** stämmig.
22 f. **impecunious:** mittellos.
23 f. **benefactor:** Wohltäter; hier: Ernährer.

gratulate myself, and I have old Mrs. Fleshman playing with the notion of the hideous Madonna. No one ever bothers to tell her that any particular piece of hers is bad, because they are all so bad. However I
5 lack your fine touch in selling to the old Jewish matrons. I can persuade them of the excellence of the investment, but you alone had the fine spiritual approach to a piece of art that unarmed them. Besides they probably never entirely trust another Jew.
10 A delightful letter came yesterday from Griselle. She writes that she is about to make me proud of my little sister. She has the lead in a new play in Vienna and the notices are excellent – her discouraging years with the small companies are beginning to bear fruit.
15 Poor child, it has not been easy for her, but she has never complained. She has a fine spirit, as well as beauty, and I hope the talent as well. She asked about you, Martin, in a very friendly way. There is no bitterness left there, for that passes quickly when one is
20 young as she is. A few years and there is only a memory of the hurt, and of course neither of you was to be blamed. Those things are like quick storms, for a moment you are drenched and blasted, and you are so wholly helpless before them. But then the sun comes,
25 and although you have neither quite forgotten, there remains only gentleness and no sorrow. You would not have had it otherwise, nor would I. I have not written Griselle that you are in Europe but perhaps I

---

2 **hideous:** abscheulich, scheußlich, grässlich.
12 **lead:** Hauptrolle.
13 **notice:** Kritik, Rezension.
23 **drenched:** durchnässt.
　 blasted: durchgeschüttelt.

shall if you think it wise, for she does not make
friends easily and I know she would be glad to feel
that friends are not far away.

Fourteen years since the war! Did you mark the
5 date? What a long way we have traveled, as peoples,
from that bitterness! Again, my dear Martin, let me
embrace you in spirit, and with the most affectionate
remembrances to Elsa and the boys, believe me,

Your ever most faithful,
10 Max

---

4 **Fourteen years since the war!:** Bezugnahme auf das Ende des
Ersten Weltkriegs 1918.
7 **affectionate:** liebevoll, herzlich.
8 **remembrances:** Empfehlungen, Grüße.

SCHLOSS RANTZENBURG
MUNICH, GERMANY

December 10, 1932

Mr. Max Eisenstein
5 Schulse-Eisenstein Galleries
San Francisco, California, U.S.A.

Max, Dear Old Fellow:

The check and accounts came through promptly,
for which my thanks. You need not send me such de-
10 tails of the business. You know how I am in accord
with your methods, and here at Munich I am in a rush
of new activities. We are established, but what a turmoil! The house, as you know, I had long in mind.
And I got it at an amazing bargain. Thirty rooms and
15 about ten acres of park; you would never believe it.
But then, you could not appreciate how poor is now
this sad land of mine. The servants' quarters, stables
and outbuildings are most extensive, and would you
believe it, we employ now ten servants for the same
20 wages of our two in the San Francisco home.

The tapestries and pieces we shipped make a rich
show and some other fine furnishings I have been
able to secure, so that we are much admired, I was
almost to say envied. Four full services in the finest

12 f. **turmoil:** Durcheinander, Aufruhr.
15 **acre:** Flächenmaß; entspricht etwa 4047 m².
21 **tapestry:** Wandteppich.

china I have bought and much crystal, as well as a full service of silver for which Elsa is in ecstasies.

And for Elsa – such a joke! You will, I know, laugh with me. I have purchased for her a huge bed. Such 5 a size as never was before, twice the bigness of a double bed, and with great posters in carved wood. The sheets I must have made to order, for there are no sheets made that could fit it. And they are of linen, the finest linen sheets. Elsa laughs and laughs, 10 and her old *Grossmutter* stands shaking her head and grumbles, "*Nein*, Martin, *nein*. You have made it so and now you must take care or she will grow to match it."

"*Ja*," says Elsa, "five more boys and I will fit it just 15 nice and snug." And she will, Max.

For the boys there are three ponies (little Karl and Wolfgang are not big enough to ride yet) and a tutor. Their German is very bad, being too much mixed with English.

20 Elsa's family do not find things so easy now. The brothers are in the professions and, while much respected, must live together in one house. To the family we seem American millionaires and while we are far from that yet our American income places us 25 among the wealthy here. The better foods are high in price and there is much political unrest even now

2 **to be in ecstasies:** überglücklich sein.
6 **great posters:** *tall posts* (vgl. *four-poster bed* ›Himmelbett‹).
   carved: geschnitzt.
11 **to grumble:** brumme(l)n, murren.
15 **snug: 1.** gemütlich, behaglich, kuschelig; **2.** haargenau, wie angegossen.
17 **tutor:** Privatlehrer.

16

under the presidency of Hindenburg, a fine liberal whom I much admire.

Already old acquaintances urge me that I interest myself in administrative matters in the town. This I take under consideration. It may be somewhat to our benefit locally if I become an official.

As for you, my good Max, we have left you alone, but you must not become a misanthrope. Get yourself at once a nice fat little wife who will busy herself with all your cares and feed you into a good humor. That is my advice and it is good, although I smile as I write it.

You write of Griselle. So she wins her success, the lovely one! I rejoice with you, although even now I resent it that she must struggle to win her way, a girl alone. She was made, as any man can see, for luxury and for devotion and the charming and beautiful life where ease allows much play of the sensibilities. A gentle, brave soul is in her dark eyes, but there is something strong as iron and very daring too. She is a woman who does nothing and gives nothing lightly. Alas, dear Max, as always, I betray myself. But although you were silent during our stormy affair, you know that the decision was not easy for me. You never reproached me, your friend, while the little sister suffered, and I have always felt you knew that I

---

1 **presidency:** Präsidentschaft.
Hindenburg: Paul von Beneckendorff und von H. (1847–1934), deutscher Reichspräsident 1925–34.
8 **misanthrope:** Misanthrop, Menschenfeind.
17 **play of the sensibilities:** Gemeint ist vermutl. *display of abilities.*
21 **alas:** ach!
to betray o.s.: sich verraten.
24 **to reproach s.o.:** jdm. Vorwürfe machen.

suffered too, most gravely. What could I do? There was Elsa and my little sons. No other decision was possible to make. Yet for Griselle I keep a tenderness that will last long after she has taken a much younger man for husband or lover. The old wound has healed but the scar throbs at times, my friend.

I wish that you will give her our address. We are such a short distance from Vienna that she can feel there is for her a home close at hand. Elsa, too, knows nothing of the old feeling between us and you know with what warmth she would welcome your sister, as she would welcome you. Yes, you must tell her that we are here and urge her to soon make a contact with us. Give her our most warm congratulations for the fine success that she is making.

Elsa asks that I send to you her love, and Heinrich would also say "hello" to Uncle Max. We do not forget you, Maxel.

My heartiest greetings to you,
Martin

6 **to throb:** pochen, schmerzen.

January 21th, 1933

Herrn Martin Schulse
5 Schloss Rantzenburg
Munich, Germany

My Dear Martin:

I was glad to forward your address to Griselle. She
should have it shortly, if she has not already received
10 it. What jollification there will be when she sees you
all! I shall be with you in spirit as heartily as if I also
could rejoin you in person.

You speak of the poverty there. Conditions have
been bad here this winter, but of course we have
15 known nothing of the privations you see in Germany.

Personally, you and I are lucky that we have such a
sound following for the gallery. Of course our own
clientele are cutting their purchases but if they buy
only half as much as before we shall be comfortable,
20 not extravagantly so, but very comfortable. The oils
you sent are excellent, and the prices are amazing. I
shall dispose of them at an appalling profit almost at
once. And the ugly Madonna is gone! Yes, to old Mrs.

---

10 **jollification:** Vergnügen, Spaß.
15 **privations:** Entbehrungen, Not.
17 **following:** Anhängerschaft, Freundes-, Kundenkreis.
20 **oils:** *oil paintings.*
22 **appalling:** fürchterlich, ungeheuer.

Fleshman. How I gasped at her perspicacity in recognizing its worth, hesitating to set a price! She suspected me of having another client, and I named an indecent figure. She pounced on it, grinning slyly as
5 she wrote her check. How I exulted as she bore the horror off with her, you alone will know.

Alas, Martin, I often am ashamed of myself for the delight I take in such meaningless little triumphs. You in Germany, with your country house and your af-
10 fluence displayed before Elsa's relatives, and I in America, gloating because I have tricked a giddy old woman into buying a monstrosity. What a fine climax for two men of forty! Is it for this we spend our lives, to scheme for money and then to strut it publicly? I
15 am always castigating myself, but I continue to do as before. Alas, we are all caught in the same mill. We are vain and we are dishonest because it is necessary to triumph over other vain und dishonest persons. If I do not sell Mrs. Fleshman our horror, somebody else will
20 sell her a worse one. We must accept these necessities.

1 **to gasp at s. th.:** sprachlos über etwas sein.
  perspicacity: Urteilsvermögen, Sachverstand.
4 **indecent:** unverschämt, horrend.
  to pounce on s. th.: sich auf etwas stürzen, bei etwas zuschlagen.
  slyly (adv.): schlau, verschlagen, gerissen.
5 **to exult:** jubeln, frohlocken.
9f. **affluence:** Wohlstand.
11 **to gloat:** sich diebisch freuen.
  giddy: verrückt, verschroben.
12 **monstrosity:** Ungetüm.
  climax: Höhepunkt, Gipfel.
14 **to strut** (infml.): zur Schau stellen.
15 **to castigate o. s.:** sich verurteilen, scharf kritisieren, geißeln.
16 **mill** (fig.): Tretmühle, Routine, Gewohnheit.

But there is another realm where we can always find something true, the fireside of a friend, where we shed our little conceits and find warmth and understanding, where small selfishnesses are impossible and
5 where wine and books and talk give a different meaning to existence. There we have made something that no falseness can touch. We are at home.

Who is this Adolf Hitler who seems rising toward power in Germany? I do not like what I read of him.
10 Embrace all the young fry and our abundant Elsa for

Your ever affectionate,
Max

---

1 **realm:** Bereich.
3 **conceits:** etwa: Allüren.
8f. **Hitler who seems rising toward power in Germany:** Die Ernennung Hitlers zum Reichskanzler am 30. Januar 1933 (vgl. Datum des Briefs) leitete den Prozess der nationalsozialistischen Machtergreifung und die sich schrittweise verschärfende Judenverfolgung ein.
10 **fry:** (Fisch-)Brut.
abundant: üppig.

March 25, 1933

Mr. Max Eisenstein
5 Schulse-Eisenstein Galleries
San Francisco, California, U.S.A.

Dear Old Max:

You have heard of course of the new events in Germany, and you will want to know how it appears to us
10 here on the inside. I tell you truly, Max, I think in many ways Hitler is good for Germany, but I am not sure. He is now the active head of the government. I doubt much that even Hindenburg could now remove him from power, as he was truly forced to place him
15 there. The man is like an electric shock, strong as only a great orator and a zealot can be. But I ask myself, is he quite sane? His brown shirt troops are of the

---

8 **new events:** Auf den Reichstagsbrand am 27. Februar 1933 folgte
einen Tag später die Notverordnung. Sie hob die wichtigsten Grund-
rechte der Weimarer Reichsverfassung auf, ermöglichte die Fest-
nahme politischer Gegner und führte für eine Reihe von Taten die
Todesstrafe ein. Durch die Annahme des verfassungsändernden
Ermächtigungsgesetzes am 23. März 1933 (vgl. Datum des Briefs)
wurden die demokratischen Parteien teils verboten, teils zur Auflö-
sung gezwungen. Damit wurde das Deutsche Reich zum Einpar-
teienstaat.

16 **orator:** Redner.
zealot: Fanatiker.

17 **sane:** geistig gesund, bei Verstand, normal.

rabble. They pillage and have started a bad Jew-baiting. But these may be minor things, the little surface scum when a big movement boils up. For I tell you, my friend, there is a surge – a surge. The people
5 everywhere have had a quickening. You feel it in the streets and shops. The old despair has been thrown aside like a forgotten coat. No longer the people wrap themselves in shame; they hope again. Perhaps there may be found an end to this poverty. Something, I do
10 not know what, will happen. A leader is found! Yet cautiously to myself I ask, a leader to where? Despair overthrown often turns us in mad directions.

Publicly, as is natural, I express no doubt. I am now an official and a worker in the new regime and I exult
15 very loud indeed. All of us officials who cherish whole skins are quick to join the National Socialists. That is the name for Herr Hitler's party. But also it is not only expedient, there is something more, a feeling that we of Germany have found our destiny and that
20 the future sweeps toward us in an overwhelming wave. We too must move. We must go with it. Even now there are being wrongs done. The storm troopers

---

1 **rabble:** Pöbel, Plebs, gemeines Volk.
   to pillage: plündern.
1 f. **Jew-baiting:** Judenhetze, -verfolgung.
3 **scum:** (Ab-)Schaum, (oben schwimmende) Schicht.
4 **surge:** (fig.) Woge, Brodeln, (große) Bewegung.
5 **quickening:** Beflügelung, Ansporn.
15 **to cherish s. th.:** etwas hegen, schätzen; für etwas sorgen.
18 **expedient:** angebracht, ratsam, nützlich, vorteilhaft, opportun.
22 **storm troopers** (pl.): Sturmabteilung, SA. Die Kampf- und Propagandatruppe der NSDAP wurde ab 1933 zur Ausschaltung des politischen Widerstands gegen die nationalsozialistische Machtergreifung eingesetzt.

are having their moment of victory, and there are bloody heads and sad hearts to show for it. But these things pass; if the end in view is right they pass and are forgotten. History writes a clean new page.

All I now ask myself, and I can say to you what I cannot say to any here is: Is the end right? Do we make for a better goal? For you know, Max, I have seen these people of my race since I came here, and I have learned what agonies they have suffered, what years of less and less bread, of leaner bodies, of the end of hope. The quicksand of despair held them, it was at their chins. Then just before they died a man came and pulled them out. All they now know is, they will not die. They are in hysteria of deliverance, almost they worship him. But whoever the savior was, they would have done the same. God grant it is a true leader and no black angel they follow so joyously. To you alone, Max, I say I do not know. I do not know. Yet I hope.

So much for politics. Ourselves, we delight in our new home and have done much entertaining. Tonight the mayor is our guest, at a dinner for twenty-eight. We spread ourselves a little, maybe, but that is to be forgiven. Elsa has a new gown of blue velvet, and is in terror for fear it will not be big enough. She is with child again. There is the way to keep a wife contented, Max. Keep her so busy with babies she has no time to fret.

---

9 **agony:** Qual.
11 **quicksand:** Treibsand.
14 **deliverance:** Rettung, Befreiung, Erlösung.
24 **gown:** elegantes Kleid.
   velvet: Samt.
27 **to fret:** beunruhigt, besorgt sein, sich aufregen, Sorgen machen.

Our Heinrich has made a social conquest. He goes
out on his pony and gets himself thrown off, and who
picks him up but the Baron Von Freische. They have
a long conversation about America, and one day the
baron calls and we have coffee. Heinrich will go there
to lunch next week. What a boy! It is too bad his German is not better but he delights everyone.

So we go, my friend, perhaps to become part of
great events, perhaps only to pursue our simple
family way, but never abandoning that trueness of
friendship of which you speak so movingly. Our
hearts go out to you across the wide sea, and when
the glasses are filled we toast "Uncle Max."

Yours in affectionate regard,
Martin

May 18, 1933

Herrn Martin Schulse
5 Schloss Rantzenburg
Munich, Germany

Dear Martin:

I am in distress at the press reports that come pour-
ing in to us from the Fatherland. Thus it is natural
10 that I turn to you for light while there are only con-
flicting stories to be had here. I am sure things cannot
be as bad as they are pictured. A terrible pogrom,
that is the consensus of our American papers.

I know your liberal mind and warm heart will tol-
15 erate no viciousness and that from you I can have the
truth. Aaron Silberman's son has just returned from
Berlin and had, I hear, a narrow escape. The tales he
tells of what he has seen, floggings, the forcing of
quarts of castor oil through clenched teeth and the
20 consequent hours of dying through the slow agony of
bursting guts, are not pretty ones. These things may

10 **light** (fig.): Aufklärung.
12 **pogrom:** Pogrom, Hetze, Ausschreitungen.
13 **consensus:** übereinstimmende Meinung.
15 **viciousness:** Skrupellosigkeit, Brutalität.
18 **flogging:** Auspeitschen.
19 **quart:** Hohlmaß; entspricht etwa einem Liter.
     castor oil: Rizinusöl.
     clenched: zusammengepresst.
21 **guts:** Eingeweide, Gedärme.

27

be true, and they may, as you have said, be but the brutal surface froth of human revolution. Alas, to us Jews they are a sad story familiar through centuries of repetition, and it is almost unbelievable that the old martyrdom must be endured in a civilized nation today. Write me, my friend, and set my mind at ease.

Griselle's play will come to a close about the end of June after a great success. She writes that she has an offer for another role in Vienna and also for a very fine one in Berlin for the autumn. She is talking most of the latter one, but I have written her to wait until the anti-Jewish feeling has abated. Of course she uses another name which is not Jewish (Eisenstein would be impossible for the stage anyway), but it is not her name that would betray her origin. Her features, her gestures, her emotional voice proclaim her a Jewess no matter what she calls herself, and if this feeling has any real strength she had best not venture into Germany just at present.

Forgive me, my friend, for so distrait and brief a letter but I cannot rest until you have reassured me. You will, I know, write in all fairness. Pray do so at once.

With the warmest protestations of faith and friendship for you and yours, I am ever your faithful

Max

---

2 **froth:** Schaum.
5 **martyrdom:** Martyrium.
12 **to abate:** sich legen, nachlassen.
16 **proclaim her a Jewess:** verraten, dass sie eine Jüdin ist.
20 **distrait:** zerstreut, konfus.
21 **to reassure:** beruhigen.
23 **protestation:** Beteuerung.

July 9, 1933

Mr. Max Eisenstein
5 Schulse-Eisenstein Galleries
San Francisco, California, U.S.A.

Dear Max:

You will see that I write upon the stationery of my
bank. This is necessary because I have a request to
10 make of you and I wish to avoid the new censorship
which is most strict. We must for the present discon-
tinue writing each other. It is impossible for me to be
in correspondence with a Jew even if it were not
that I have an official position to maintain. If a com-
15 munication becomes necessary you must enclose it
with the bank draft and not write to me at my house
again.

As for the stern measures that so distress you, I
myself did not like them at first, but I have come to
20 see their painful necessity. The Jewish race is a sore
spot to any nation that harbors it. I have never hated
the individual Jew – yourself I have always cherished
as a friend, but you will know that I speak in all hon-

---

10 **censorship:** (staatliche) Zensur.
16 **bank draft:** Bankscheck, -anweisung.
18 **stern:** strikt, scharf, streng.
20 f. **sore spot:** wunder Punkt, heikles Thema; Übel, ständiges Ärgernis.

esty when I say I have loved you, not because of your race but in spite of it.

The Jew is the universal scapegoat. This does not happen without reason, and it is not the old super-
5 stition about "Christ-killers" that makes them distrusted. But this Jew trouble is only an incident. Something bigger is happening.

If I could show you, if I could make you see – the rebirth of this new Germany under our Gentle
10 Leader! Not for always can the world grind a great people down in subjugation. In defeat for fourteen years we bowed our heads. We ate the bitter bread of shame and drank the thin gruel of poverty. But now we are free men. We rise in our might and hold our
15 heads up before the nations. We purge our bloodstream of its baser elements. We go singing through our valleys with strong muscles tingling for a new work – and from the mountains ring the voices of Wodan and Thor, the old, strong gods of the German
20 race.

But no. I am sure as I write, as with the new vision my own enthusiasm burns, that you will not see how

---

3 **scapegoat:** Sündenbock.
10f. **to grind s. o. down:** jdn. zermürben, aufreiben.
11 **subjugation:** Unterjochung, (sklavische) Abhängigkeit.
13 **gruel:** Haferschleim.
15 **to purge:** reinigen.
17 **to tingle:** zittern, beben.
19 **Wodan:** in der germanischen Mythologie Herr und König der Götter und Menschen; sieghafter Kämpfer und Gott der Schlachten.
   Thor: altnordischer Name des germanischen Gottes Donar, der die Macht über Winde und Wolken besitzt; neben Wodan bedeutendste und gewaltigste Gestalt der germanischen Mythologie.

necessary is all this for Germany. You will see only
that your own people are troubled. You will not see
that a few must suffer for the millions to be saved.
You will be a Jew first and wail for your people. This I
understand. It is the Semitic character. You lament
but you are never brave enough to fight back. That is
why there are pogroms.

Alas, Max, this will pain you, I know, but you must
realize the truth. There are movements far bigger
than the men who make them up. As for me, I am a
part of the movement. Heinrich is an officer in the
boys' corps which is headed by Baron Von Freische
whose rank is now shedding a luster upon our house,
for he comes often to visit with Heinrich and Elsa,
whom he much admires. Myself, I am up to the ears
in work. Elsa concerns herself little with politics except to adore our Gentle Leader. She gets tired too
easily this last month. Perhaps the babies come too
fast. It will be better for her when this one is born.

I regret our correspondence must close this way,
Max. Perhaps we can someday meet again on a field
of better understanding.

As ever your,
Martin Schulse

4 **to wail for s. o.:** um jdn. klagen.
13 **luster:** Glanz.
14 **to visit with s. o.** (infml.): sich mit jdm. unterhalten.
17 **to adore:** verehren, über alles lieben.

August 1, 1933

Herrn Martin Schulse
5 (kindness of J. Lederer)
Schloss Rantzenburg
Munich, Germany

Martin, My Old Friend:

I am sending this by the hand of Jimmy Lederer, who
10 will shortly pass through Munich on a European va-
cation. I cannot rest after the letter you last sent me. It
is so unlike you I can only attribute its contents to your
fear of the censorship. The man I have loved as a
brother, whose heart has ever been brimming with sym-
15 pathy and friendship, cannot possibly partake of even a
passive partnership in the butchery of innocent people.
I trust and pray that it may be so, that you will write me
no exposition, which might be dangerous for you, –
only a simple "yes." That will tell me that you play the
20 part of expediency but that your heart has not changed,
and that I was not deluded in believing you to be always
a man of fine and liberal spirit to whom wrongs are
wrongs in whosoever's name they may be committed.

---

5 **kindness:** (durch) freundliche Unterstützung, Vermittlung.
15 **to partake of s.th.:** an etwas teilhaben, beteiligt sein.
18 **exposition:** Erläuterung, Kommentar.
20 **expediency:** Opportunität; hier auch: Opportunismus.
21 **to be deluded in believing …:** fehlgehen in der Annahme, dass …

33

This censorship, this persecution of all men of liberal thought, the burning of libraries and corruption of the universities would arouse your antagonism if there had been no finger laid on one of my race in Germany. You are a liberal, Martin. You have always taken the long view. I know that you cannot be swept away from sanity by a popular movement which has so much that is bad about it, no matter how strong it may be.

I can see why the Germans acclaim Hitler. They react against the very real wrongs which have been laid on them since the disaster of the war. But you, Martin, have been almost an American since the war. I know that it is not my friend who has written to me, that it will prove to have been only the voice of caution and expediency.

Eagerly I await the one word that will set my heart at peace. Write your "yes" quickly.

My love to you all,
Max

---

1 **persecution:** Verfolgung.
3 **antagonism:** Feindseligkeit, Ablehnung.
5f. **to take the long view:** Weitblick haben, die Folgen bedenken.
6f. **sanity:** Vernunft, Verstand.
9 **to acclaim s.o.:** jdm. zujubeln, Beifall spenden.

Deutsch-Völkische Bank und Handelsgesellschaft,
München

August 18, 1933

Mr. Max Eisenstein
5 Schulse-Eisenstein Galleries
San Francisco, California, U.S.A.

Dear Max:

I have your letter. The word is "no." You are a
sentimentalist. You do not know that all men are not
10 cut to your pattern. You put nice little tags on them,
like "liberal" and expect them to act so-and-so. But
you are wrong. So, I am an American liberal? No! I
am a German patriot.

A liberal is a man who does not believe in doing
15 anything. He is a talker about the rights of man, but
just a talker. He likes to make a big noise about
freedom of speech, and what is freedom of speech?
Just the chance to sit firmly on the backside and say
that whatever is being done by the active men is
20 wrong. What is so futile as the liberal? I know him
well because I have been one. He condemns the
passive government because it makes no change. But
let a powerful man arise, let an active man start to
make a change, then where is your liberal? He is

10 **tag:** Schildchen, Etikett.
15f. **to be just a talker** (infml.): immer nur reden.
20 **futile:** zum Scheitern verurteilt.

against it. To the liberal any change is the wrong one.

He calls this the "long view," but it is merely a bad scare that he will have to do something himself. He 5 loves words and high-sounding precepts but he is useless to the men who make the world what it is. These are the only important men, the doers. And here in Germany a doer has risen. A vital man is changing things. The whole tide of a people's life changes in a 10 minute because the man of action has come. And I join him. I am not just swept along by a current. The useless life that was all talk and no accomplishment I drop. I put my back and shoulders behind the great new movement. I am a man because I act. Before that 15 I am just a voice. I do not question the ends of our action. It is not necessary. I know it is good because it is so vital. Men are not drawn into bad things with so much joy and eagerness.

You say we persecute men of liberal thought, we 20 destroy libraries. You should wake from your musty sentimentalizing. Does the surgeon spare the cancer because he must cut to remove it? We are cruel. Of course we are cruel. As all birth is brutal, so is this new birth of ours. But we rejoice. Germany lifts high 25 her head among the nations of the world. She follows her Glorious Leader to triumph. What can you know of this, you who only sit and dream? You have never

---

5 **precept:** Grundsatz, Prinzip.
7 **doer:** Tatmensch, jd., der entschlossen handelt.
15 **I am:** *I was.*
19 **to persecute:** verfolgen.
20 **musty:** verstaubt, altmodisch.

known a Hitler. He is a drawn sword. He is a white light, but hot as the sun of a new day.

I must insist that you write no further. We are no longer in sympathy, as now we must both realize.

Martin Schulse

September 5, 1933

Herrn Martin Schulse
5 c/o Deutsch-Voelkische Bank
und Handelsgesellschaft
Munich, Germany

Dear Martin:

Enclosed are your draft and the month's accounts.
10 It is of necessity that I send a brief message. Griselle
has gone to Berlin. She is too daring. But she has
waited so long for success she will not relinquish it,
and laughs at my fears. She will be at the Koenig The-
ater. You are an official. For old friendship's sake, I
15 beg of you to watch over her. Go to Berlin if you can
and see whether she is in danger.

It will distress you to observe that I have been
obliged to remove your name from the firm's
name. You know who our principal clients are, and
20 they will touch nothing now from a firm with a German name.

Your new attitude I cannot discuss. But you must
understand me. I did not expect you would take up
arms for my people because they are my people, but
25 because you were a man who loved justice.

---

12 **to relinquish s. th.:** auf etwas verzichten.

I commend my rash Griselle to you. The child does not realize what a risk she is taking. I shall not write again.

Goodbye, my friend,

Max

---

1 **to commend:** anvertrauen, in Obhut geben.
rash: unbesonnen, unvorsichtig.

November 5, 1933

Herrn Martin Schulse
5 c/o Deutsch-Voelkische Bank
und Handelsgesellschaft
Munich, Germany

Martin:

I write again because I must. A black foreboding
10 has taken possession of me. I wrote Griselle as soon
as I knew she was in Berlin and she answered briefly.
Rehearsals were going brilliantly; the play would
open shortly. My second letter was more encourage-
ment than warning, and it has been returned to me,
15 the envelope unopened, marked only addressee unknown, (*Adressant Unbekannt*). What a darkness
those words carry! How can she be unknown? It is
surely a message that she has come to harm. They
know what has happened to her, those stamped
20 letters say, but I am not to know. She has gone into
some sort of void and it will be useless to seek her.
All this they tell me in two words, *Adressant Unbekannt.*

---

3 **November 5, 1933:** Im Oktober 1933 trat Deutschland aus der Ab-
rüstungskonferenz und dem Völkerbund aus.

9 **foreboding:** Vorahnung, ungutes Gefühl.

15 **addressee:** Adressat.

21 **void:** Leere, Nichts.

Martin, need I ask you to find her, to succor her? You have known her graciousness, her beauty and sweetness. You have had her love, which she has given to no other man. Do not attempt to write to me.
5 I know I need not even ask you to aid. It is enough to tell you that something has gone wrong, that she must be in danger.

I leave her in your hands, for I am helpless.

Max

---

1 **to succor:** helfen, beistehen.
2 **graciousness:** Freundlichkeit, Liebenswürdigkeit; Güte; Anmut.

November 23, 1933

Herrn Martin Schulse
5 ℅ Deutsch-Voelkische Bank
und Handelsgeselschaft
Munich, Germany

Martin:

I turn to you in despair. I could not wait for an-
10 other month to pass so I am sending some in-
formation as to your investments. You may wish to
make some changes and I can thus enclose my appeal
with a bank letter.

It is Griselle. For two months there has been only
15 silence from her, and now the rumors begin to come
in to me. From Jewish mouth to Jewish mouth the
tales slowly come back from Germany, tales so full
of dread I would close my ears if I dared, but I cannot. I must know what has happened to her. I must
20 be sure.

She appeared in the Berlin play for a week. Then
she was jeered from the audience as a Jewess. She is
so headstrong, so foolhardy, the splendid child! She

---

22 **to jeer s. o.:** jdn. verhöhnen.
23 **headstrong:** eigensinnig, dickköpfig.
    foolhardy: wagemutig.

threw the word back in their teeth. She told them proudly that she *was* a Jewess.

Some of the audience started after her. She ran backstage. Someone must have helped her for she got away with the whole pack at her heels and took refuge with a Jewish family in a cellar for several days. After that she changed her appearance as much as she could and started south, hoping to walk back to Vienna. She did not dare try the railroads. She told those she left that she would be safe if she could reach friends in Munich. That is my hope, that she has gone to you, for she has never reached Vienna. Send me word, Martin, and if she has not come there make a quiet investigation if you can. My mind cannot rest. I torture myself by day and by night, seeing the brave little thing trudging all those long miles through hostile country, with winter coming on. God grant you can send me a word of relief.

Max

---

1 **to throw s.th. back in s.o.'s teeth** (fig.): Variante zu *to throw s.th. back in s.o.'s face* ›jdm. etwas heimzahlen‹.

5f. **to take refuge with s.o.:** Zuflucht bei jdm. finden.

12f. **to send s.o. word:** jdm. Nachricht geben.

16 **to trudge:** stapfen, sich schleppen.

Deutsch-Völkische Bank und Handelsgesellschaft,
München

December 8, 1933

Heil Hitler! I much regret that I have bad news for
you. Your sister is dead. Unfortunately she was, as
you have said, very much a fool. Not quite a week
ago she came here, with a bunch of storm troopers
right behind her. The house was very active – Elsa has
not been well since little Adolf was born last month –
the doctor was here, and two nurses, with all the servants and children scurrying around.

By luck I answer the door. At first I think it is an
old woman and then I see the face, and then I see the
storm troopers have turned in the park gates. Can I
hide her? It is one chance in thousands. A servant will
be on us at any minute. Can I endure to have my
house ransacked with Elsa ill in bed and to risk being
arrested for harboring a Jew and to lose all I have
built up here? Of course as a German I have one
plain duty. She has displayed her Jewish body on the
stage before pure young German men. I should hold
her and turn her over to the storm troopers. But this I
cannot do.

"You will destroy us all, Griselle," I tell her. "You
must run back further in the park." She looks at me

---

8 **active:** Gemeint ist *busy*.
11 **to scurry:** huschen.
17 **to ransack s.th.:** etwas durchsuchen.
18 **to harbor s.o.:** jdm. Unterschlupf gewähren, jdn. verstecken.

45

and smiles (she was always a brave girl) and makes her own choice.

"I would not bring you harm, Martin," she says, and she runs down the steps and out toward the trees.
5 But she must be tired. She does not run very fast and the storm troopers have caught sight of her. I am helpless. I go in the house and in a few minutes she stops screaming, and in the morning I have the body sent down to the village for burial. She was a fool to
10 come to Germany. Poor little Griselle. I grieve with you, but as you see, I was helpless to aid her.

I must now demand you do not write again. Every word that comes to the house is now censored, and I cannot tell how soon they may start to open the mail
15 to the bank. And I will no longer have any dealings with Jews, except for the receipt of money. It is not so good for me that a Jewess came here for refuge, and no further association can be tolerated.

A new Germany is being shaped here. We will soon
20 show the world great things under our Glorious Leader.

Martin

---

13 **to censor s. th.:** etwas zensieren, der Zensur unterwerfen.

CABLEGRAM

MUNICH JANUARY 2 1934

MARTIN SCHULSE

YOUR TERMS ACCEPTED NOVEMBER TWELVE
5 AUDIT SHOWS THIRTEEN PERCENT INCREASE
FEBRUARY SECOND FOURFOLD ASSURED PAN
EXHIBITION MAY FIRST PREPARE LEAVE FOR
MOSCOW IF MARKET OPENS UNEXPECTEDLY
FINANCIAL INSTRUCTIONS MAILED NEW AD-
10 DRESS

EISENSTEIN

---

1 **cablegram:** Telegramm.
5 **audit:** Revision, Rechnungs-, Bilanzprüfung.
6 **fourfold** (adv.): vierfach.
  pan: Gesamt-, Gemeinschafts-, international.

EISENSTEIN GALLERIES
SAN FRANCISCO, CALIFORNIA, U.S.A.

January 3, 1934

Herrn Martin Schulse
5 Schloss Rantzenburg
Munich, Germany

Our Dear Martin:

Don't forget grandma's birthday. She will be 64 on
the 8th. American contributors will furnish 1,000
10 brushes for your German Young Painters' League.
Mandelberg has joined in supporting the league. You
must send 11 Picasso reproductions, 20 by 90 to
branch galleries on the 25th, no sooner. Reds and
blues must predominate. We can allow you $ 8,000 on
15 this transaction at present. Start new accounts book 2.
Our prayers follow you daily, dear brother,

Eisenstein

---

9 **contributor:** Spender.
14 **to predominate:** dominieren, überwiegen.

January 17, 1934

Herrn Martin Schulse
Schloss Rantzenburg
Munich, Germany

Martin, Dear Brother:

Good news! Our stock reached 116 five days ago.
The Fleishmans have advanced another $ 10,000. This
will fill your Young Painters' League quota for a
month but let us know if opportunities increase. Swiss
miniatures are having a vogue. You must watch the
market and plan to be in Zurich after May first if any
unexpected opportunities develop. Uncle Solomon
will be glad to see you and I know you will rely
heavily on his judgment.

The weather is clear and there is little danger of
storms during the next two months. You will prepare
for your students the following reproductions: Van
Gogh 15 by 103, red; Poussin 20 by 90, blue and yellow; Vermeer 11 by 33, red and blue.

Our hopes will follow your new efforts.   Eisenstein

---

10 **quota:** Bedarf.

12 **to have a vogue:** gerade in Mode, sehr populär sein.

20 **Poussin: 1.** Nicolas P. (1594–1665), französischer Maler; **2.** Gaspard
P., d. i. G. Dughet (um 1615–75), französischer Maler, Schwager und
Schüler von Nicolas Poussin, dessen Namen er mitunter führte.

21 **Vermeer:** Jan V., genannt V. van Delft (um 1632–75), niederländi-
scher Maler und Kunsthändler.

EISENSTEIN GALLERIES
SAN FRANCISCO, CALIFORNIA, U.S.A.

January 29, 1934

Dear Martin:

5   Your last letter was delivered by mistake at
457 Geary St., Room 4. Aunt Rheba says tell Martin
he must write more briefly and clearly so his friends
can understand all that he says. I am sure everyone
will be in readiness for your family reunion on the
10 15th. You will be tired after these festivities and may
want to take your family with you on your trip to Zurich.

Before leaving however, procure the following reproductions for branches of German Young Painters'
15 League, looking forward to the joint exhibit in May
or earlier: Picasso 17 by 81, red; Van Gogh 5 by 42,
white; Rubens 15 by 204, blue and yellow.

Our prayers are with you.

Eisenstein

13 **to procure:** beschaffen, erwerben.

SCHLOSS RANTZENBURG
MUNICH, GERMANY

February 12, 1934

Mr. Max Eisenstein
Eisenstein Galleries
San Francisco, California, U.S.A.

Max, My Old Friend:

My God, Max, do you know what you do? I shall
have to try to smuggle this letter out with an American I have met here. I write an appeal from a despair
you cannot imagine. This crazy cable! These letters
you have sent. I am called in to account for them. The
letters are not delivered, but they bring me in and
show me letters from you and demand I give them
the code. A code? And how can you, a friend of long
years, do this to me?

Do you realize, have you any idea that you destroy
me? Already the results of your madness are terrible.
I am bluntly told I must resign my office. Heinrich is
no longer in the boys' corps. They tell him it will not
be good for his health. God in heaven, Max, do you
see what that means? And Elsa, to whom I dare not
tell anything, comes in bewildered that the officials
refuse her invitations and Baron Von Freische does
not speak to her upon the street.

Yes, yes, I know why you do it – but do you not
understand I could do nothing? What could I have
done? I did not dare to try. I beg of you, not for my-

self, but for Elsa and the boys – think what it means
to them if I am taken away and they do not know if I
live or die. Do you know what it is to be taken to a
concentration camp? Would you stand me against a
5 wall and level the gun? I beg of you, stop. Stop now,
while everything is not yet destroyed. I am in fear for
my life, for my life, Max.

Is it you who does this? It cannot be you. I have
loved you like a brother, my old Maxel. My God,
10 have you no mercy? I beg you, Max, no more, no
more! Stop while I can be saved. From a heart filled
with old affection I ask it.

Martin

EISENSTEIN GALLERIES
SAN FRANCISCO, CALIFORNIA, U.S.A.

February 15, 1934

Herrn Martin Schulse
Schloss Rantzenburg
Munich, Germany

Our Dear Martin:

Seven inches of rainfall here in 18 days. What a season! A shipment of 1,500 brushes should reach the
Berlin branch for your painters by this weekend. This will allow time for practice before the big exhibition. American patrons will help with all the artists' supplies that can be provided, but you must make the final arrangements. We are too far out of touch with the European market and you are in a position to gauge the extent of support such a showing would arouse in Germany. Prepare these for distribution by March 24th: Rubens 12 by 77, blue; Giotto 1 by 317, green and white; Poussin 20 by 90, red and white.

Young Blum left last Friday with the Picasso specifications. He will leave oils in Hamburg and Leipzig and will then place himself at your disposal.

Success to you!
Eisenstein

---

16 **to gauge:** ermessen, beurteilen.
18 **Giotto:** G. di Bondone (1266–1337), italienischer Maler und Baumeister.
20f. **specifications:** genaue Angaben.

EISENSTEIN GALLERIES
SAN FRANCISCO, CALIFORNIA, U.S.A.

March 3, 1934

Martin Our Brother:

Cousin Julius has two nine-pound boys. The family is happy. We regard the success of your coming artists' exhibition as assured. The last shipment of canvases was delayed due to difficulties of international exchange but will reach your Berlin associates in plenty of time. Consider reproduction collection complete. Your best support should come from Picasso enthusiasts but neglect no other lines.

We leave all final plans to your discretion but urge an early date for wholly successful exhibit.

The God of Moses be at your right hand.

Eisenstein

7f. **canvas:** Leinwand; Ölgemälde (auf Leinwand).
13 **to leave s. th. to s. o.'s discretion:** etwas in jds. Ermessen stellen, jds. Entscheidung überlassen.

EISENSTEIN GALLERIES

SAN FRANCISCO, CALIFORNIA, U.S.A.

Mr. Martin Schulse
Schloss Rantzenburg
Munich

G E R M A N Y

Adressat unbekannt

Editorische Notiz

Der englische Text folgt der Ausgabe: Kathrine Kressmann Taylor, *Address Unknown*, New York: Washington Square Press, 2001. Das Glossar erklärt in der Regel alle Wörter, die nicht in *Reclams Englischem Wörterbuch* von Dieter Hamblock (Stuttgart: Reclam, 1996) verzeichnet sind.

Der vorliegende Briefwechsel weist des Öfteren soziolektal geprägte Ausdrücke und Formulierungen des jeweiligen Verfassers auf. Es ist daher mit Abweichungen von der englischen Standardsprache vor allem im Bereich der Syntax, Verbformen und Wortwahl zu rechnen. Die entsprechenden Wörter und Wendungen wurden jedoch nur im Falle gravierender, zu möglichen Verständnisschwierigkeiten führender Irregularitäten kommentiert. Offensichtliche Rechtschreibfehler im Deutschen wurden nicht korrigiert.

Im Glossar verwendete Abkürzungen

adv.	adverb
fig.	figuratively (übertragen)
infml.	informal (umgangssprachlich)
o. s.	oneself
pl.	plural
s. o.	someone
s. th.	something

Inhalt